PICTURE THAT

A Century Of Cork

Memories

Compiled and Edited by **Stephen Coughlan**

Publisher: **John Coughlan**
Designed by **Dara Ó Lochlainn**
Cover photograph hand-tinted by **Amelia Stein**
Photographs © **Examiner Publications (Cork) Limited**

An Examiner Publication

Research: **Walter McGrath, Deirdre Higgins, Louise Coughlan, Dan Linehan**

Typesetting by **Fingerprint**
Origination by **Litho Colour Plates**
Printed by **ColourBooks** in the Republic of Ireland.

First Published 1985
This edition Published 1996

The following is a list of the photographers who over the decades contributed to the Cork Examiner Picture Library:

Tom Barker Snr., John O'Keefe, Tommy O'Brien, Tom Barker, Louis McMonagle, Michael O' Kelly, Roy Hammond, Cyril Perrott, Sean Horgan, Michael Minihane, Richard Mills, Donal Sheehan, Michael Olney, Des Barry, Denis Scannell, Denis Minihane, Eddie O'Hare, Maurice O'Mahony, Paddy Barker and Dan Linehan.

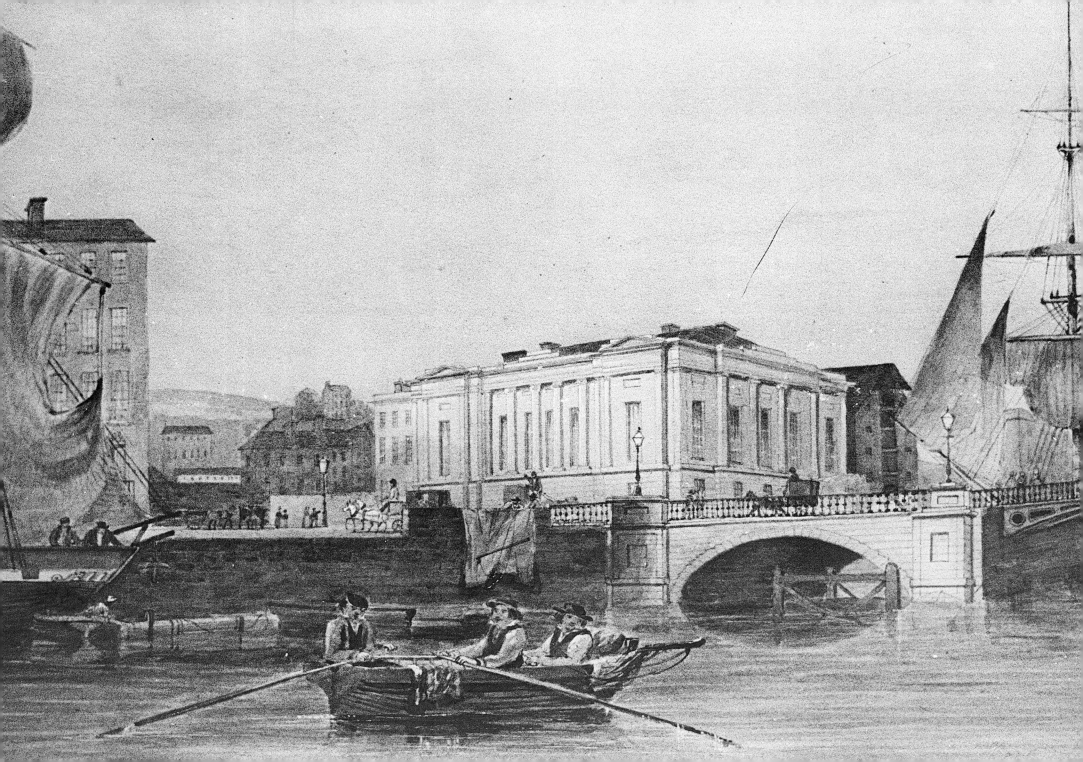

Foreword

Opposite: A painting of the Cork Savings Bank Building in the days of sail. This picture now hangs in the board room of the Cork Savings Bank.

The century-old photographic archives of the Cork Examiner contain a unique collection of negatives. This newspaper was one of the first to employ a full time press photographer —Thomas Barker — away back in the early 1900's. As the century progressed, and certainly from the late 1920's onwards, the filing and cataloguing of plates was done with great care, thus ensuring that these priceless records were preserved for future generations.

The Examiner is proud of its collection, because of the immense variety of news material and the fact that something like 120,000 glass negatives are stored in such a manner as to make it possible for future research to be carried out amongst its treasures.

Our Editorial Director Donal Crosbie felt that the 800 celebrations of our City's Charter provided a very valid reason for sharing these pictorial gems with our readers, so the historical "Goldmine" was opened up and the treasures revealed.

He asked me to organise an exhibition and subsequently this publication, "Picture That". The exhibition was staged in the Crawford Municipal Gallery, Cork, for a three-week period and drew a record attendance of 25,000.

The task of publishing this collection of "Pictures of the Past" was made immeasurably easier because it was done in association with the Cork Trustee Savings Bank, another veteran institution of our city. The Bank opened for business on December 20, 1817, in a room at the Cork Institution. Business days consisted of only two per week including Saturday from 12.30 to 2.30. No deposit of less than 10 pence was to be received and interest was at the rate of 4 per cent. The bank flourished and moved to new premises in Pembroke Street in 1824.

Then in 1839 two years before the Cork Examiner was born, Sir Thomas Deane and his brother, Mr. Kearns Deane designed the magnificent building with frontages on Lapps Quay and Warren's Place (now Parnell Place). It cost £11,000 and opened on August 20th 1842. It stands today as a monument to two distinguished Cork architects whose work can be seen in many public buildings in the city. The bank now has branches all over Munster.

And so the Cork Examiner (established in 1841) and the Cork Trustee Savings Bank have united to promote this unique publication with a view to reviving old memories and recalling the life and times of Corkonians who lived in decades long past.

Stephen Coughlan

July 1985

Time passes on and in doing so it creates changes in lives and institutions. So has it been with the two principles mentioned in the 1985 foreword of the original edition of this book.

Donal Crosbie died on 10th March, 1990, and is remembered in the Donal Crosbie Memorial Library in the "Examiner" office, Academy Street.

Stephen Coughlan died on the 17th January, 1994, and this new edition of "Picture That" is his memorial.

Finally on 29th March, 1996, "The Cork Examiner" became "The Examiner" and continues to thrive in its wider role.

Ted Crosbie
Executive Chairman
Examiner Publications (Cork) Limited.

July 1996

Contents

6

The Archibald Russell, one of the last of the windjammers, arrives in Cork with a cargo of grain from Australia. Our picture, taken about 50 years ago, shows the s.s. Shark owned by Palmers, Ringaskiddy, towing the graceful sailing vessel to her berth in the upper reaches of the River Lee.▷

Tall ships at Cork Quays.

The Falls of Garry — A spectacular picture of a stately windjammer which went aground near the Sovereign Islands off Oysterhaven, County Cork in 1911.

Historic day at the North Mon — Unveiling of a memorial bust of the late Rev. Br. Burke.

Patrick Street 1901 — Read all the latest on the Transvaal Crisis in the Examiner. ▷

Firemen's Rest hut in Patrick Street, Cork with the ever-present fire ladder was for many years a feature of life in the city centre. Times change and modern fire-fighting equipment did away with the necessity for random fire points of which there were a number strategically placed in Cork. The Patrick Street hut is now occupied by C.I.E. staff. The fire-ladder has long disappeared. Older residents of St. Lukes Cross will recall a similar fire fighting unit in that area.

An interior view of the Weigh House in the Old Cork Butter Market neath Shandon steeple. Butter from here was exported all over the world and much of the city's prosperity stemmed from the Dairy industry in Munster.

In the early years of the century Lambkins tobacco factory in Fishers Street Merchant's Quay, Cork, was thriving. These fascinating pictures of the ladies sorting tobacco leaves and another group packing tins were taken during the first World War. The tins were for dispatch to front line troops and it was said that the ladies often packed a love message in the tins!

The Parnell Drum & Fife Band on parade in Cork in early years of the century.

Social Life of the Smithy — The blacksmith's forge was the place for much gossip and socialising as well as for the serious business of fitting horseshoes. ▷

This picture taken about 1914 shows one of the new railway bridges open for river traffic. Carmichael Hall is at left of picture and the Coliseum Cinema at the corner of McCurtain St. had not yet been built.

Horse Fair in early 1900's — A horse fair in progress in the grounds of the old Corn Exchange, Anglesea Street, Cork. In the background are some coaches of the Cork Bandon and South Coast Railway in Albert Quay station.

It is over 80 years since this picture was taken near the Marina on the occasion of a seaside excursion for children. Lord Mayor Augustine Roche is giving them some advice before they set out on the journey. ▷

Cork Park Race Course which closed down in 1917 to make way for the Ford car plant. The site was later shared with Dunlops, the E.S.B., Gouldings Fertiliser factory and smaller industries. Both Ford and Dunlop closed their factories within the past few years.

For many years St. Monica's Home, Infirmary Road, Cork catered for the blind. This picture taken in the early years of the century shows the residents at work on basket making. The Home closed down some years ago.

South Channel 1915 — The distant spire of Holy Trinity church is one of the few surviving landmarks from this view of the old Municipal Buildings and Parnell Bridge about 1915.

It was bonfire night in the "Marsh" the "flat of Cork City" when this picture was taken many decades ago.

In the early and more leisurely days of the century the Sunday excursion was frequently by Wagonette and here we see a party leaving Merchants Quay for a day trip.

A scene at Canon Sheehan's funeral in Doneraile in 1913. The priest was one of the most prolific writers of the era.

18

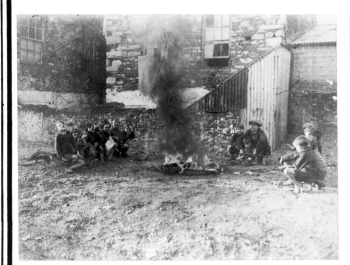

The first and only lady Freemason, Elizabeth St. Leger, was inducted into Masonry in Doneraile Court, Co. Cork in the seventeenth century. She fell asleep in the alcove pictured here, and when she awoke a Lodge was in progress in an adjoining room. She heard the secret ceremonial so had to be inducted a Mason! She is buried in St. Finbarr's Cathedral, Cork.

Churchill at the Blarney Stone — Whether one admired Sir Winston Churchill's political activities or not, there was no denying that he was one of the world's greatest orators. Did kissing the Blarney Stone improve his gift of eloquence? Here he is seen about to perform the kissing exploit in 1912. ▷

20

Honouring Brian Dillon — A picture from Dillon's Cross, Cork in 1909 when the original plaque on the home of the old Fenian, Brian Dillon, was unveiled. The house was burned during the troubled time of 1920, and later a new house and plaque erected.

This was the first plane to land in Cork. It was piloted by Lord Carbery who is seen here (left) with his mechanic, on the Mardyke, Cork. The citizens enjoyed their first close-up view of a "Flying Machine".

Skating on the Lough in the winter of 1912.

Lord Mayor Henry O'Shea hosts a party for the ceremony of the throwing of the dart in Cork Harbour in 1915. The practice was discontinued many years ago, probably because champagne became too expensive. ▷

Tomas MacCurtain, the murdered Lord Mayor of Cork, lying in state in 1920.

Colmans Lane

Broad Lane

Broad Lane from North Main Street.

Trimbaths Lane

Broad Lane from Broad Street
(Below)

27

St. Joseph's Court

Cross Lane

New Fair Lane (Below)

Off Paul Street

Moriartys Lane

Shaws Alley off Back Street

In the early years of World War I Irish recruits for the British army were well catered for before they left for the Front. Volunteer Committees were set up to provide comforts for the fighting men.

The First World War — Men of an Irish regiment entraining at Glanmire Road station during the 1914-18 Great War. ▷

O'Leary's Lane, now O'Leary's Place at the top of Barrack Street. Note St. Finbarrs Cathedral in the background.

A dispatch rider of 1915 on a belt-driven, single-cylinder-
engined motor cycle, thought to be either a BSA or Triumph.
The belt was leather — and notorious for slipping in wet
weather.

Recruiting For Great War — A regimental band adds to the
ardour of the recruiting campaign in Cork in the early years of
World War I. ▷

The British Fleet pictured at Castletownbere in 1912.

32

British troops pull out from Victoria, later Collins, Barracks.

The Union Jack Down — Scene in Victoria Barracks, Cork (now Collins Barracks) as the British hand over to Irish troops in 1921.

No doubt there were a few survivors of the Fenian Rising of 1867 among this "Old Guard" of the Irish Republican Brotherhood marching in a Manchester Martyrs procession in Cork in the 1920's. In centre is Lord Mayor Sean French, who was Cork's First Citizen 1924/31 and 1933/37.

Belgian refugees fleeing from the advancing German armies found refuge in this country in 1915. They are seen here in Cork with the Lord Mayor, Sir Henry O'Shea who helped to arrange succour and comfort for the visitors through a number of charitable organisations. ▷

The Lord Mayor of Cork Terence McSwiney who died on hunger strike in Brixton Prison 1920 lying in state in Cork City Hall.

This is not the place to revive the bitter memories of the Anglo/Irish fighting of 1920/21. But one of the most savage events in Cork's history was the malicious burning by crown forces of much of the city centre and the City Hall on December 12, 1920, following the ambushing of some British troops at Dillons Cross. We reproduce here some pictures which give an idea of the extent of the havoc.

Armoured Railcars in Cork — In 1922-23 when the anti-Treaty forces inflicted much damage to Ireland's railways, the new Free State Army formed a special Railway Repair and Defence Corps. Here are some of its members with two of their armoured railcars at Cork station. ▷

A Barracks In Ruins — One of the earliest aerial pictures in the Cork Examiner files is this one of Ballincollig, Co. Cork Military Barracks (now Murphy Barracks) after it had been burned in the Civil War 1922. In the distance can be seen part of the former powdermills.

This railway bridge near Ballincollig was a casualty of the Civil War back in 1922. ▷

Cork's old City Hall, destroyed in the burning of Cork in 1920 by the Black & Tans.

Repairs to Rochestown Viaduct — Members of the Free State Army's Railway Repair and Defence Corps working at mined Rochestown Viaduct of the Cork Blackrock and Passage Railway during the Civil War. The bridge has recently (1984-85) become part of a scenic municipal walk.

Western Road 1922 — An early stage of the funeral of General Michael Collins after the tragic ambush at Beal na Blath, Co. Cork. ▷

Mallow Bridge Blown Up — An action carried out by the IRA in 1922 during the Civil War.

42

The White Star liner Titanic seen in Cork Harbour before setting out on her ill-fated voyage to the U.S. on April 11, 1912. Two days out of Cobh she struck an iceberg and sank with the loss of two thirds of the 2,358 passengers and crew. The stern view shows Roches Point at the mouth of Cork Harbour.

44

Survivors from the Cunard liner Lusitania torpedoed by a German submarine twelve miles off the Old Head of Kinsale.

The Liner Lusitania was torpedoed by a German submarine on May 7, 1915. She sank within 18 minutes and 1,200 passengers and crew were drowned. Many of the victims were buried in Cobh (then Queenstown).

46

An appeal for the Lifeboat Association was an elaborate effort in the late 1920's and '30's. Here in Patrick Street, Cork, was this attractive tableau designed to highlight the needs of the men who risk their lives around our coast.

The famed "Muskerry" Crash — The scene near Carrigrohane on September 6, 1927, when a steamroller working on the surfacing of the Carrigrohane Straight Road crashed into the morning train from Donoughmore of the Cork and Muskerry Light Railway. The cause of the accident was never explained but local wags held that the steamroller and train were having a race! Nobody was seriously injured but several lady passengers fainted. ▷

48

This Model-T Ford came off second best when it collided with a tram at Tivoli, Cork. In the 1920's and '30's members of the Garda Siochana wore a helmet similar to that of Britain's constabulary.

Dalys suspension bridge which spans the Lee between Sunday's Well and the Mardyke was officially opened in February 1927 by Mr C. O'Driscoll and James Daly, a city businessman who contributed a great deal to the cost of the bridge.

Glum expressions on the Lady Elsie. The steamer plied between Bantry, Glengarrif and Berehaven up to 1940. ▷
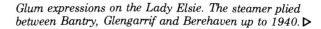

50

Ronnie Palmer & Richard (Dickie) Wallace operated a fleet of famous excursion ships in Cork Harbour for many years. The vessels also doubled as tenders serving the liners which visited Cork Harbour regularly. Such names as the Failte, the Saorstat, the Morsecock and the Duke of Devonshire will be familiar to the old generations. Dickie Wallace was for many years Chairman of the Cork Harbour Board.

Over The Viaduct — Chetwynd Viaduct near Cork, built in 1850-51, bore the West Cork trains for 110 years until the service ceased in 1961. Now only the gaunt remains of the fine structure survive.

A busy shopping scene in Patrick Street, Cork, about 1928. Note the old motorcars. ▷

A three-horse team at work reaping and binding on a farm in Carrigtwohill, Co. Cork, in September 1930.

The Passage West, Co. Cork Fire Brigade display their new horse drawn equipment in 1913. Standing near the horses is Fire Chief Capt. Roberts who was a grandson of Capt. Richard Roberts, skipper of the Sirius, first steamer to cross the Atlantic.

Cork's Efficient Fire Brigade — When this picture was taken in the late 1920's outside the old Sullivan's Quay fire station, the solid-wheeled fire engine was the last word in modern fire fighting equipment. ▷

On December 12, 1928, the White Star liner, Celtic, ran aground off Roches Point in Cork Harbour. No lives were lost but the vessel was eventually broken up and sold off as salvage.

The Guileen Coast Life Rescue crew at Roches Point following the wreck of the liner Celtic in 1928. The old horse drawn vehicle is still preserved.

Unloading a steamer at Lapps Quay.

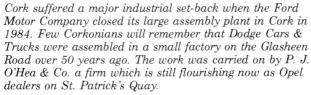

Cork suffered a major industrial set-back when the Ford Motor Company closed its large assembly plant in Cork in 1984. Few Corkonians will remember that Dodge Cars & Trucks were assembled in a small factory on the Glasheen Road over 50 years ago. The work was carried on by P. J. O'Hea & Co. a firm which is still flourishing now as Opel dealers on St. Patrick's Quay.

Cork Distilleries Company was very proud of its new "fleet" acquired in 1929. "Paddy Flaherty" whiskey, named after one of the company's most successful travellers was for generations one of the areas most popular brews and still is, even though all the major Irish Distilleries have since amalgamated. As will be seen by our picture, taken on Morrison's Island, the brand name was shortened to "Paddy" after a period.

The Old Entrance to UCC — Only students who were strong swimmers made it to class the day the river swept the bridge away.

U.C.C. Dairy Science Block — Mr. W. T. Cosgrave, President of the Executive Council of the Irish Free State, laying the foundation stone of the U.C.C. Dairy Science Building in July, 1928. ▷

The little fishing village of Blackrock outside Cork City was the setting each year for the Blessing of the nets. Alas, times have changed and fishing has declined as Blackrock began to grow into a major suburb of the city. This picture was taken almost 60 years ago.

An old-time threshing scene on a Carrigtwohill farm in Co. Cork. ▷

One Horse-Power Railway — An interesting survival right into the 1960's was the siding from the Clonakilty branch of West Cork's railways to Shannonvale flour mills, near Ballinascarthy. "Paddy", the motive power, could haul two wagons at a time through a scenic half-mile siding to the junction with the Clonakilty line where locomotives took over. This picture was taken in 1954. The line was once featured on British TV. It closed, March 1961.

Anticipation — before the advent of motor traffic the Horse trough was a familiar object to Cork City people. Today only a few remain and the water supply has long dried up. This picture was taken in the 1920's. The trough survives.

"Cabbage and Queens" on Cork's famous Coal Quay Market about 1928: ▷

"You wouldn't believe it" — down through the years the anglers have amused and entertained their friends with accounts of the size and antics of the "one that got away".

64

Golf pics from the "Good Old Days".

Cahirmee's Famous Fair — A picture from the 1930's of the famous Cahirmee horse fair in Buttevant. The fair attracted hundreds of travelling people.

View of Brian Boru Street, the Coliseum corner and Trinity Presbyterian Church which show varied examples of the motorised vehicles of the 1930's, but the most interesting feature is the herd of pigs being driven through the city. One can just imagine the traffic chaos they would cause in the same location, 40 or 50 years later. ▷

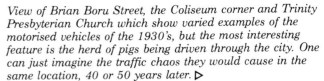

Danny Hobbs a well-known Cork comedian and Master of his own pack of hounds, gives a helping hand to a young follower. The picture was taken about 50 years ago.

Tom O'Neill renowned exponent of the sport of road bowling, a game peculiar to Cork and Armagh, attempts to "loft" the Chetwynd Viaduct which carried the West Cork Railway line up to 1961.

Travelling People at the Cahirmee Fair many years ago. ▷

Seal shooting along the rugged Rennies coast not far from the picturesque and ancient town of Kinsale, Co. Cork in 1934.

This corner of George's Quay near Parliament Bridge was a traditional market place on Fridays for the fish sellers. The ladies specialised in sprats which were sold for a few pence per handful. The fishermen brought their loaded boats up to the slipway near the bridge.

A scene on Cork's Cornmarket Street some thirty years ago. The shawl was a much favoured mode of dress up to the 1950's. Today Cornmarket Street is still a bustling trading place beloved of local bargain hunters. It is often mis-named the "Coal Quay", which is some distance away. ▷

72

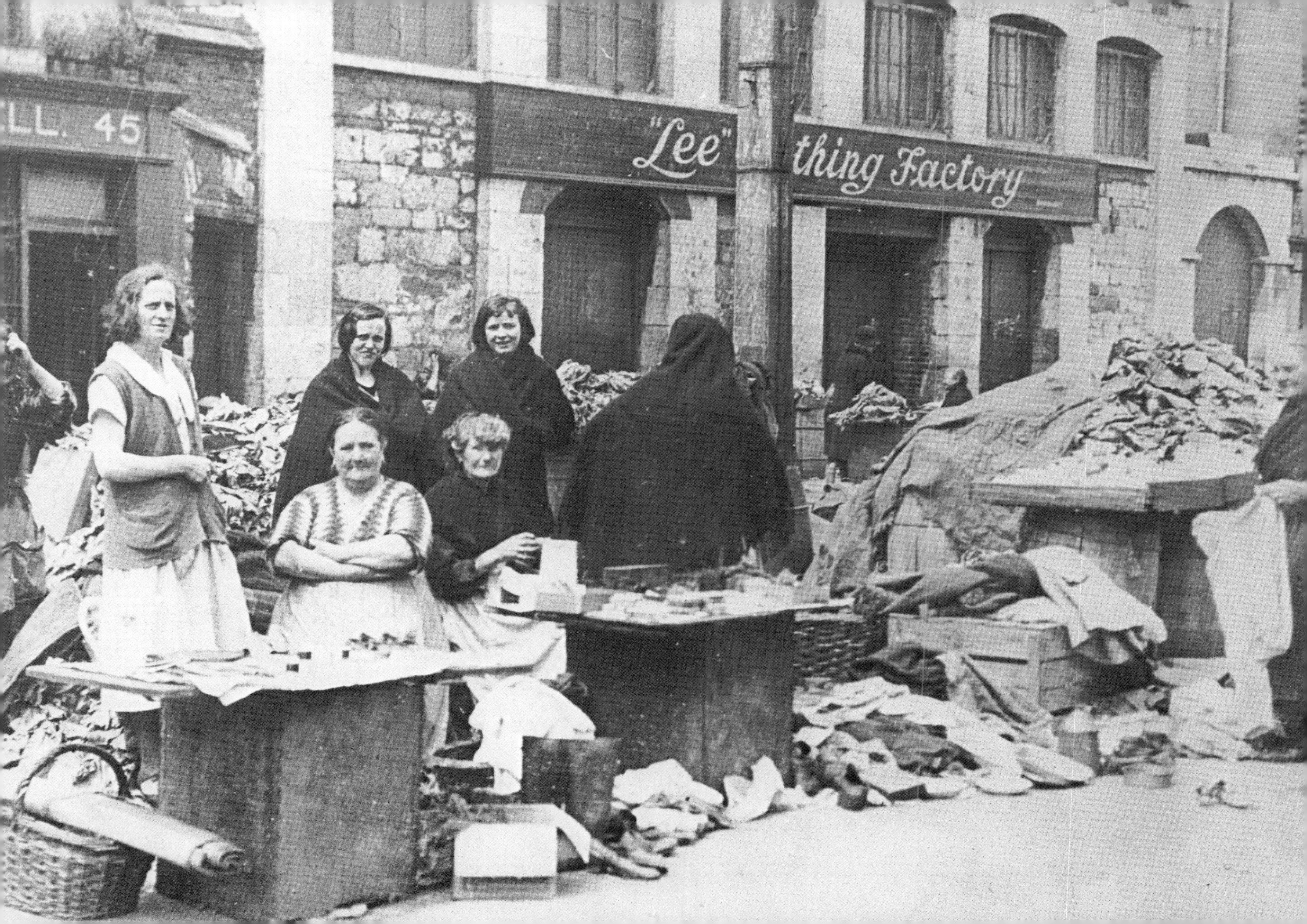

LL. 45
"Lee" thing Factory

Cork Transport

First Electric Railway — This quaint picture (copy from our files) shows a primitive "tramcar" operating at the Christian Brothers Exhibition in the Corn Exchange, Anglesea St., Cork, in 1889. It was built by two pioneer electricians, Brother Dominic Burke (North Monastery) and Gerald Percival. ▷

The covered cars in the foreground of this old picture of Patrick Street were very popular in Cork in the first quarter of the century.

Trams Lined Up at Statue — Not a strike of tramwaymen, but an occasion in 1920 when all the drivers and conductors left the trams lined up at the Fr. Mathew Statue and marched to the Cathedral to pray for Lord Mayor Terence MacSwiney, then dying on hunger strike in Brixton Prison. The same scene was captured by an early cine cameraman and it appears in the George Morrison film "Mise Eire".

By Tram To Salthill — About 1910 Cork Examiner cameraman Thomas Barker was in Galway and took this picture of the Salthill horse-tram in Eyre Square. The tramway closed about 1919.

The Renard Road Train — Bumpy, but you got there in the end. ▷

Muskerry Tram Near Its End — Competing with buses and cars for roadway space the "Muskerry Tram" (formerly Cork and Muskerry Light Railway) is seen here on Western Road near College Gates only a few months before its closure in December, 1934.

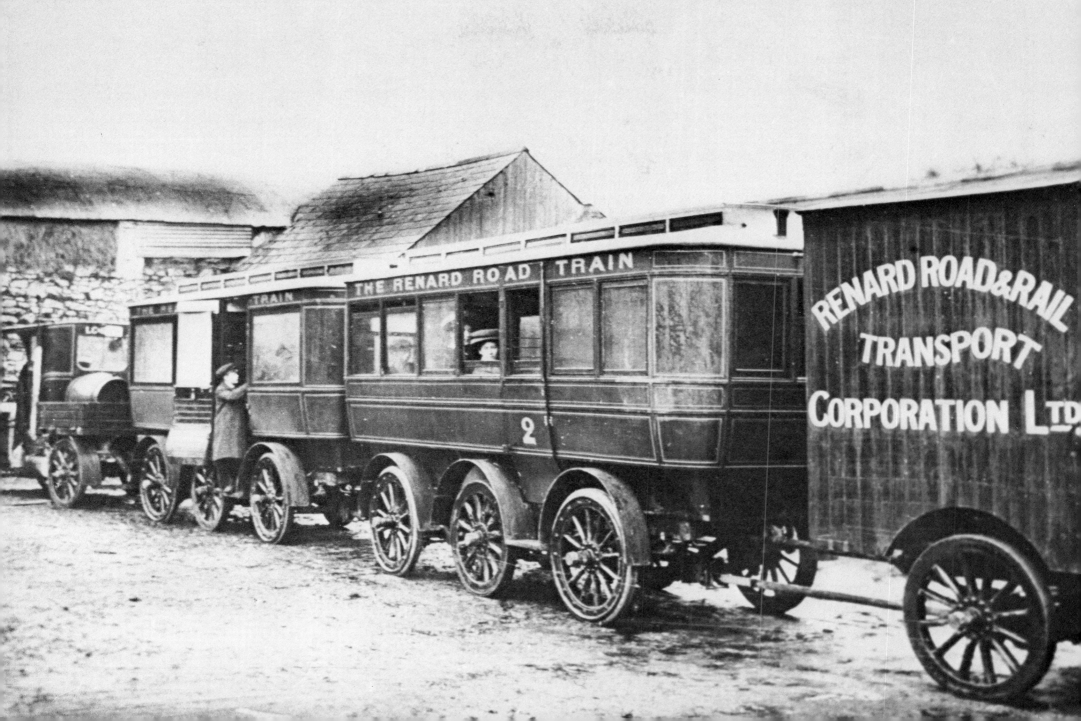

The Charabanc was a popular mode of transport in the 1920's and a regular service operated between Cork and Ballycotton. This picture was taken on the Old Blackrock Road and was apparently an outing for some members of the British Forces.

Mobility and Grandeur — These early "motorists" were ▷ obviously of the wealthy class. They sacrificed nothing in dignity or comfort in their travels — provided the day was fine.

Farewell To West Cork Railways — Hired by the Irish Railway Record Society for a farewell tour of West Cork railways just before their closure in March 1961, immaculately groomed locomotive No. 464 of the old Cork Bandon and South Coast Railway enters Albert Quay station greeted by many railway enthusiasts.

In the late 1920's a sleeper bus operated between Cork and Dublin. It did not attract the patronage expected by the operating company and was withdrawn after a short period. It is seen here outside the Victoria Hotel, in Patrick Street, prior to setting out for Dublin.

In the old days when there were few cars on the roads, the steam trains brought thousands of visitors to Youghal during the summer months. It s spacious strand was one of Cork's favourite resorts. ▷

The crew gather around the engine (one of the surviving locomotives of the old Waterford Limerick and Western Railway) on the last livestock train from Macroom Fair in November 1953. This was the end of the Macroom Railway.

This picture was taken in the late 1930's and it shows the change in motor vehicles over the intervening years. The old Parnell Bridge has long since been replaced by a spacious four lane structure.

With Shandon Steeple in the background, Cattle Avenue presents a typical Cork Northside scene of the 1920's. ▷

Unloading a steamer at the Cork Quays in the 1930's.

The South Union Hunt meet at the Fingerpost in Douglas, Cork, in 1930. A vast change has taken place in this location over the years and a major roundabout now guides the heavy motor traffic at this busy urban junction.

In 1937 the ice-cream cart was a popular feature of sports meetings and matches. Here the youthful sportsmen take time off to enjoy a luscious cone. ▷

A pleasant setting for sports day in Macroom, Co. Cork in 1933. The ruined castle was demolished in later years.

Two little Cork girls erect a shrine on Kyrl's Quay to honour a religious occasion in 1935.

Civic Dignitaries from Cork pictured in Dublin in 1932 for the Eucharistic Congress

Riverside Carnival and Regatta was an annual event which drew thousands of spectators. Our picture was taken in 1936. The event has long since lapsed. ▷

The liner Ile de France at anchor off Cobh. It was described as Paris afloat.

When they repaved Patrick St. the old timber setts made excellent firewood. Hence this scramble. ▷

The submarine Nautilus which was towed into Cork in June 1931 on a voyage from the U.S. to Britain. The distinguished explorer Sir Hubert Wilkins planned to sail under the arctic ice to the North Pole. The expedition was abandoned after the submarine had got to within 500 miles of the Pole.

88

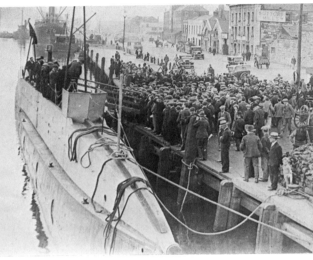

They Couldn't Swim There Now! — The start of the Tivoli Reclamation Scheme (later the cross-channel ferry berth site) with many Cork youngsters enjoying a dip in the then unpolluted waters of the Lee. ▷

In 1938 Chic Acosta, a renowned U.S. swimming coach, was in Cork to conduct a training session at the Eglinton Street Baths. He is seen here putting his charges through their strokes.

Miss Mercedes Gleitze, a channel swimmer who broke the world endurance record, swimming for 30 hours in the Eglinton Street baths, Cork, in January 1930. Mr P. J. Weldon, President of the Munster Swimming Branch, Irish Swimming Association, is on her right, and Ald. Sean French, Lord Mayor of Cork, on her left.

The daring young man atop of an aircraft wing of one of Cobhams Aerial Circus during a performance in Ballincollig away back in 1934.

In the 1930's money was scarce but sporting members of the public who wanted to see a soccer match in the Mardyke grounds in Cork had a two-tier solution to the problem. ▷

Cobhams Aerial Circus was in Cork in 1933 and for many of the citizens it presented an opportunity for a first flight. This picture was taken in Ballincollig where spectacular stunts were performed to thrill the crowds which came to enjoy the unusual entertainment.

It's Fair Day in Mitchelstown, Co. Cork.

Happy Nights at Arcadia — A happy throng in Arcadia Ballroom, Cork in the mid-1930's with Pat Crowley's Band in the background (leading banjoist Joe McGinnity at extreme left). Romance was always in the air at Arcadia. ▷

Cork Grocers fancy dress cycle parade on Cork's Grand Parade about 50 years ago.

Fashion at the races in the 1920-30's.

The Battle of the Band Stand — A timeless winter scene at the Mardyke, Cork in 1930. ▷

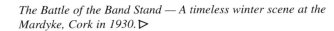

This little boy solved his transport problems of the pre-war years when he harnessed a goat to a specially-designed cart.

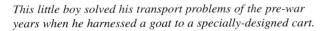

96

Danno Mahony in 1935 when home in Ballydehob, West Cork, from the U.S. where he had become a World Wrestling champion. He was noted for his "Irish Whip" a formidable throw which brought him to victory on many occasions. In November 1950 he died in a road accident near Portlaoise while on his way to Cork.

J. S. Wright who set a new world motorcycle speed record in 1932 on the Carrigrohane Road.

98

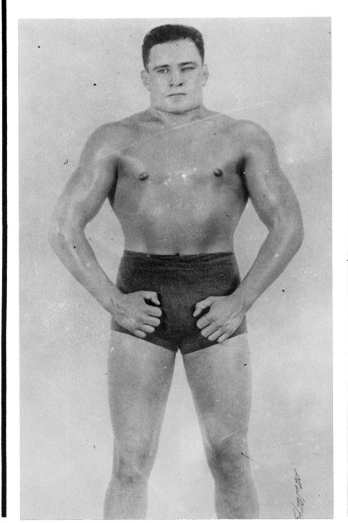

International Car Races — In the 1930's racing drivers of international renown competed in the Cork car races around the Inchigaggin — Carrigrohane — Victoria Circuit. Here are two views about 1936 at Poulavone "Hairpin Bend" (where a traffic island has been recently constructed) and at Victoria Cross.

Christmas Scenes Half a Century Ago — Fine scenes of domestic happiness and excitement in the Cork of the early 1930s. Custom has not changed very much.

The Christmas turkey market on the Grand Parade, Cork, was an occasion for bargaining. The little boy on the right of this picture, taken in 1935, didn't show much appreciation of the birds. ▷

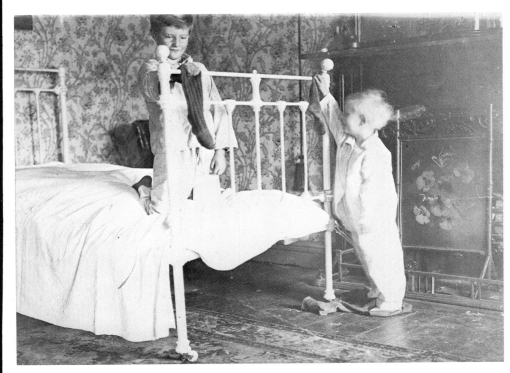

The short-Mayo Composite Aircraft at Foynes Co. Limerick, July 1938. The duo flew the first commercial crossing of the Atlantic. After take-off the Mercury separated from the mother ship to fly to Montreal.

The Kinsale cloak has all but disappeared. But when this picture was taken the ladies were still proud of their traditional and distinctive costume. ▷

The Annual Eucharistic procession in Bandon, Co. Cork wends its way up the steep flight of steps that leads to St. Patrick's Church, a beautiful edifice which dominates the town.

102

German Seaplane in Cork Harbour — St. Colman's Cathedral looks down on a German seaplane in the waters of Cobh about 1936.

This famous photograph has been reproduced many times and always arouses great interest. It shows An Taoiseach, Eamon de Valera, in Cobh for the official takeover from the British of the Cork Harbour forts in July 1938. The forts, at Spike, Camden, Carlisle and Templebreedy, had been retained by the British up to then under the terms of the Anglo-Irish Treaty of 1921. Group includes Seamus Fitzgerald H.C., Frank Aiken, Dr. Jim Ryan, Oscar Traynor, P. J. Rutledge, Lt. Vivion de Valera, Hugo Flinn, Kevin Boland etc.▷

Fr Augustine Hayden of Cork ministered to the Volunteers in the G.P.O. Dublin in 1916. He was a close friend of Eamonn de Valera.

Members of the Maritime Inscription on board the training ship Isalt Cobh, in December, 1943. The group, some of whom became well known personalities, including Bob Geldoff, father of Bob of Boomtown Rats fame, and Judge Sean Mac D. Fawsitt.

Some time after the Cork Harbour forts had been transferred from British to Irish control in July 1938, it was discovered that one of the big artillery guns in Templebreedy Fort, Crosshaven, was defective. The British government sent a replacement gun. It was too big to be unloaded at Crosshaven and had to be brought to Cork city, from where it was hauled through the streets and on to Crosshaven by steam traction engine. Our pictures, taken at Southern Road, illustrate some of the problems encountered.

This street artist on Patrick's Bridge Cork was a familiar figure to Corkonians in the 1940's.

108

Historic Day in Camden Fort — Shortly after the Cork Harbour forts were taken over by the Irish Government from the British in July 1938 Bishop Daniel Cohalan of Cork came to celebrate Mass in the garrison chapel at Camden Fort (now Dun Ui Mheachair), Crosshaven. At rear is well-known Cork Examiner journalist, John O'Sullivan. ▷

Irish Shipping Ltd. Casualty — One of many dramatic pictures taken on the East Cork coast when the Irish Plane was wrecked off Ballyshane, near Ballycotton in 1947.

Towards the end of World War Two the country suffered from a severe fuel shortage. The adverse weather conditions in 1944 necessitated an all-out effort to harvest our bogs and the army were called in to help. Our pictures taken in a Co. Cork bog show troops of the Southern Command enjoying their first experience as turf cutters.

The late Fr. Seamus O'Floinn founder of the Cork Shakespearian Society based in the "Loft" near St. Mary's Cathedral. He inspired many young men and women to interest themselves in speech & drama. His work was so successful that the B.B.C. featured him in their series "This is my Line". He served for a long period in the Cathedral Parish and later was appointed P.P. of Passage West where he continued to interest himself in the promotion of the dramatic arts. He was beloved by the children

After the fire — all that remained of the Cork Opera House which was destroyed on the night of the 12th of December 1955 ▷

Making Hay — British film star Dawn Adams, who died in 1985, takes time off from the Cork Film Festival back in 1950.

112

Gen. Dwight Eisenhower visited Ireland in August 1962. He is pictured here on the tender serving the liner America in Cobh chatting to Cobh Baggage Man "Sharkey" Griffin who served under him on the Normandy Beaches on "D" day.

The Taoiseach, Mr Jack Lynch greets President de Gaulle on arrival at Cork Airport in 1969 for a holiday in Kerry.

Ex-President Dwight Eisenhower of the U.S. visited Ireland in August 1962. On his way to join the liner America at Cobh, he was treated to a display of Irish dancing in Cobh Railway Station. With him are Mr. P. O'Mahony, Chairman of Cobh UDC and Miss Veronica Hartland UDC. The dancers were: Irene Clarke (now Mrs Jim McKenna) and Liz Keogh. ▷

114

This delightful rural scene was taken by Cork Examiner District Photographer Michael Minnihane away back in 1961. The setting was Hare Island which lies close to the West Cork coast at Cunnemore near Skibbereen. Donkey Power is very efficient in this small and beautiful island which is still populated and is popular with visitors in the Summer period.

Kennedy on Military Road — After he had landed by helicopter in Collins Barracks, Cork, during his Irish visit in June 1963 one of the earliest pictures of President John F. Kennedy's triumphal procession to the City Hall was taken here on Military Road just outside the barracks gate. ▷

Pictured at the opening of Cork Airport in October 1961 are
An Taoiseach, Mr Sean Lemass; Mr Erskine Childers and the
Lord Mayor of Cork, Mr Anthony Barry and Mrs Barry.

Famous Comedians in Cork — Oliver Hardy and Stan
Laurel being greeted by Lord Mayor Pa McGrath T.D. at the
City Hall, Cork, in the 1950's. ▷

Jim "Tough" Barry the famous trainer of the Cork hurling
team, pictured in the 1960's.

In January 1979 more than 50 people died when the French tanker Betel Geuse blew up while discharging her cargo at the Whiddy Island oil terminal in Bantry, Co. Cork.

On August 9, 1980 the death toll was 18 when the Dublin-Cork train was derailed at The Bethelgeuse Co. Cork. ▷

Siamsa Cois Laoi — Cork's own music festival of the 1980's, featuring Irish and international recording stars, attracts up to 40,000 people to Pairc Ui Chaoimh each summer.

Tragedy Again — Examiner photographer Denis Minihane took this poignant picture of 131 bodies laid out in the Regional Hospital, Cork following the Air India crash off the Kerry coast in June 1985. A total of 329 people lost their lives. ▷

Patrick Street 1985 — The transport and styles have certainly changed.

The Palace Theatre in McCurtain Street, Cork was in the early days of the century one of the city's popular centres for Variety. Back in November, 1927 this troupe of performing midgets got themselves photographed with a well-known Pointsman in Bridge Street. The Civic Guards (now Garda Siochana) in the early years of their existence wore helmets similar to those worn by the British "Bobby". The Palace was all plush and elegant with boxes for the wealthier patrons. The proscinium pictured here complete with advertising screen was ornate and beautiful. The Theatre was converted to a cinema many years ago, but it still retains several of its attractive features.

124

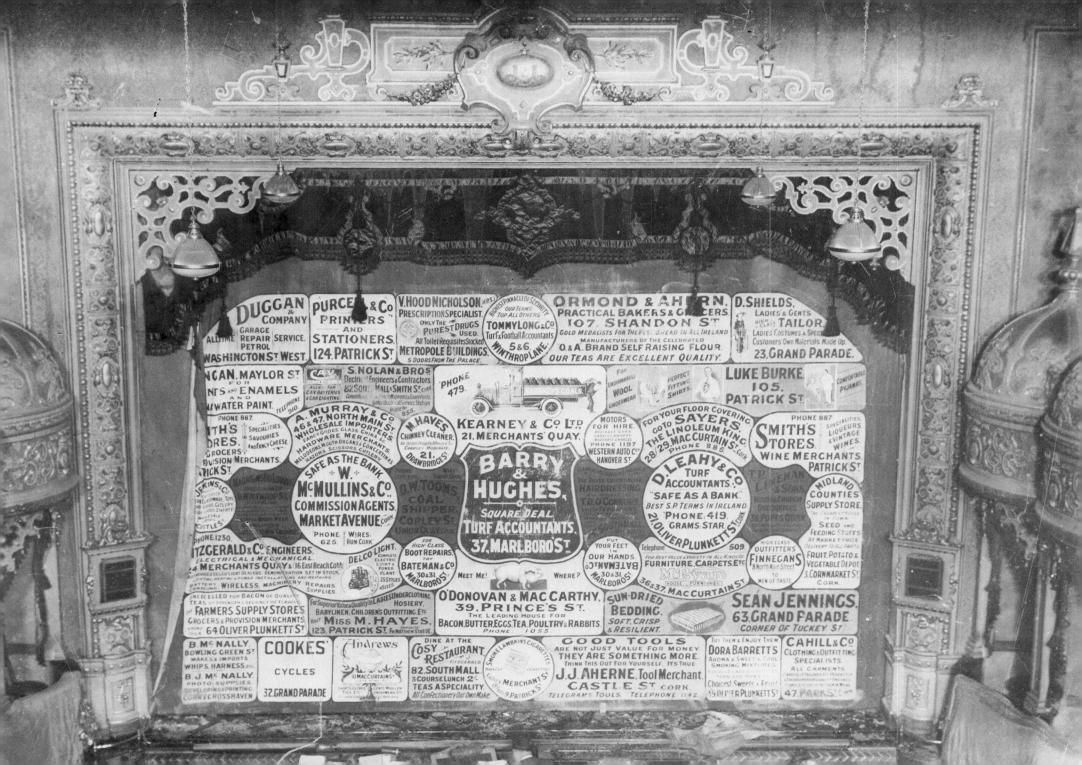

Shopfronts of Yesteryear